BUT IT WAS AN IMPORTANT FAILURE

OMAR SABBAGH

Cinnamon Press
:: small miracles from distinctive voices ::

Published by Cinnamon Press, Meirion House. Tanygrisiau, Blaenau Ffestiniog, Gwynedd, LL41 3SU www.cinnamonpress.com
The right of Omar Sabbagh to be identified as author of this work has been asserted by him in accordance with the Copyright, Designs and Patent Act, 1988.
Copyright © 2020 Omar Sabbagh. ISBN: 978-1-78864-072-5
British Library Cataloguing in Publication Data. A CIP record for this book can be obtained from the British Library.
All rights reserved. No part of this publication may be reproduced, stored in a retrieval system, or transmitted in any form or by any means, electronic, mechanical, photocopying, recording or otherwise without the prior written permission of the publishers. This book may not be lent, hired out, resold or otherwise disposed of by way of trade in any form of binding or cover other than that in which it is published, without the prior consent of the publishers.
Designed and typeset in Palatino by Cinnamon Press. Printed in Poland.
Cover design by Adam Craig.
Cinnamon Press is represented in the UK by Inpress Ltd and in Wales by the Welsh Books Council.

Acknowledgements

The author would like to thank the editors of the following magazines, journals and/or edited volumes, in which many of these poems, or earlier versions of such, have appeared previously: *Agenda* ('His Solitude'; *'Loving Vincent'*; *'Valedictions'*; 'Dawn Music, Dubai'); (T&F) *New Writing* ('The Pledge'; 'Toyless'); *Two Thirds North 2018* ('A Theory of Guilt'; 'Her Expertise'); *Two Thirds North 2019* ('The Dark Blue House Of The World'); *Reeds from Red Lips* ('The Nile Farewell'); *New Humanist* ('White Noise'); *Acumen* ('A Daughter'); *Envoi* ('General Knowledge: An Elegy'; 'On Digging'; 'Heartbeat'); *Spear's Magazine* ('A Building's Weave').
The author is grateful to the publishers and estates of poets for permission to quote from the following:
Robert Skidelsky, *John Maynard Keynes: 1883-1946: Economist, Philosopher, Statesman*, 2013.
W.H. Auden, from 'Musée Des Beaux Arts' in *Another Time* (1st ed), Faber & Faber, 1940.
Seamus Heaney, from 'The Blackbird of Glanmore' in *District and Circle*, (1st ed), Faber & Faber, 2006.
T.S. Eliot, from 'Tradition and the Individual Talent' in *The Selected Essays*, (Main Edition), Faber & Faber,1999.
Robert Graves, 'The Thieves' in *The Complete Poems*, (New Ed ed), Beryl Graves & Dunstan Ward (eds), Carcanet, 2003.

About the Author

Omar Sabbagh is a widely published poet, writer and critic. His first collection and his fourth collection are, respectively: *My Only Ever Oedipal Complaint* and *To The Middle of Love* (Cinnamon Press, 2010/17). His Beirut novella, *Via Negativa: A Parable of Exile*, was published with Liquorice Fish Books in March 2016; and a riveting collection of short fictions, *Dye and Other Stories*, was released in September 2017. His Dubai novella, *Minutes from the Miracle City* is published with Fairlight Books (July 2019); and a study of the oeuvre of Professor Fiona Sampson, *For the Love of Music* is forthcoming with Anthem Press in 2020. He has published scholarly essays on George Eliot, Ford Madox Ford, G.K. Chesterton, Henry Miller, Lawrence Durrell, Joseph Conrad, Lytton Strachey, T.S. Eliot, Basil Bunting, Hilaire Belloc, George Steiner, and others; as well as on many contemporary poets. Many of these works are collated in, *To My Mind, Or, Kinbotes: Essays on Literature*, published with Whisk(e)y Tit in 2019. He holds a BA in PPE from Oxford; three MA's, all from the University of London, in English Literature, Creative Writing and Philosophy; and a PhD in English Literature from KCL. He was Visiting Assistant Professor of English and Creative Writing at the American University of Beirut (AUB), from 2011-2013. He now teaches at the American University in Dubai (AUD), where he is Associate Professor of English.

Contents

Foreword:
    A Pretentious Man   11

Prologue:
    Writing On The Wall   17

Disenchantments And Valedictions:
    A Theory of Guilt   21
    Toyless   22
    The Dark Blue House Of The World   23
    King   24
    Her Expertise   25
    Questioning Luck, Or, Retrodiction   26
    The Mansion Of My Youth   27
    His Solitude   28
    The Chants Within Him   29
    Valedictions:
        Goodbye to All That   30
        Parade's End   31
    Pangloss   32
    Greybeard   33
    Dawn Music, Dubai   34
    Cowardice At The Confessional   35
    The Desert   36
    The Evil Eye   37

Love Songs And White Goddesses:
    The Nile Farewell   41
    The Pledge   42

Loving Vincent	43
The Woman Hungers For Drama,...	44
Three Sonnets For Faten:	
The Positive Sum	45
Her Reading Glasses	46
Loving Puritans	47
Adeodatus	46
The Silent Oryx	48
Heartbeat	50
A Daughter	51
The Ballerina	52

Reflections:

White Noise	57
Beirut Rain	58
General Knowledge: An Elegy	59
On Digging	60
Father To Father	61
Two Edifices:	
1 A Building's Weave	62
2 EMBA	64
Delusions	65
Guessing At A World	66
Growing Up	68

Epilogue:

The Clown And The Philosopher	71

Afterword:

My Practice of Poetry, Or, Not Bad	75

For Faten
Wife, Lover, Friend

And for
Alia

But It Was
An Important Failure

'On the grass when I arrive,

In the ivy when I leave.'

Seamus Heaney, 'The Blackbird of Glanmore'

'This is perhaps the characteristic of his age which separates it most strikingly from our own. It is not so much that we have lost our beliefs as that we have lost the belief in the possibility of having true beliefs.'

Robert Skidelsky, *John Maynard Keynes*

'But for him it was not an important failure…'

W.H. Auden, 'Musée Des Beaux Arts'

Foreword

A Pretentious Man

It had always been his ambition to be recognised; but how so, why so, well, those are tart questions. There was a hunger in him that was either toxic or noxious, or both. He knew it was there, hankering, harrowing, harrying. And each day, he peered down into that pool of black mercury and saw a different variation on the same dire theme, reflection. Of course, it amused him, tickled his precious mindset, affected the affectations of his refined, prone temperament, to think of the nice and nuanced way in which that term, 'reflection', held multifarious burdens; it was a word whose sinew did more than one kind of muscular work. There was the sense of mirroring of course, allowing the object-world to shore up a tender part of him; and there was the notion of thinking-on, thinking-through; there was also the more etymological sense of looking-back, what Hegel would have dubbed, probably in Finlay's translation, 'looking-on'—which latter sense most probably might be construed, and quite nicely, to conjoin the two previous, material and mental, while still holding, or beholding as it were, a third, at least a third, which though obvious to the cultivated reader shall remain implicit here in the interests of good taste and elegance. However, though he was often seen as a pretentious man, he knew himself to be merely pompous. One could of course be quite over-full and overborne with the frills of self-importance, while still knowing, in the workaday phrase, 'what one was talking about.' But perhaps there was some grain there, or here, to comb and sift? You could still be construed as pretentious by being pompous. Pretentious about yourself perhaps? Without necessarily being rightly averred 'pretentious' about what it was you said or wrote, as deemed by galleys of no doubt know-it-all's who flung the accusation, daily, or nightly; nightly with the shade or shadow of obliquity, or obtuseness, or nightly with the dark of the intent to wound no matter what.

What most irritated him, and/or what he knew was enacted by his surroundings to most irritate him, was the way the galleys in question would pick up on some reference he might use now and then, or repeatedly, and make it the sole source of his thinking-on, thinking-through. Like most bright sparks, he had his favourites, shooting stars who were just faster in the oceanic dome of his intellectual firmament; they peopled the labyrinthine halls and the maze-like, maze-neat nooks and crannies, too, of his bibliophilic mind with more force than others. They were his exponential flowers, most fecund because most returned-to. Usually it was because they, these happy working thinkers, happened to write well, white on sky-black, as much black printed matter on a white or off-white page. And that meant, all things being equal, they knew how to think in the emphatic sense of that pivotal verb, which in Yusuf's book meant they knew how to think in a meaningful way that was also incisive, and often enough polymorphous-ly so. Was it not Sir Thomas Browne who'd dubbed the rampant bibliophilic tendency as a form of 'gentle madness'? Maybe it was, maybe it wasn't (and maybe it was, maybe it wasn't). He'd only ever dipped into a volume of collated selected works of that metaphysical, so to pinion the citation with any more bluster would be mendacious. Besides, the true source of his knowledge of that phrase, 'a gentle madness', came from the title, embossed in golden print, of a far more contemporary work, a big, chunky hardback tome, whose theme was such love of books; so that to cite Sir Thomas Browne, even in his mind, was pushing it. No, that hedged; it would be, it would have been, pretentious.

All this rigmarole had gotten jumpstarted in his gifted, bilious mind, because his wife, Maryam had now been on the backend, twice or thrice in the last hour of phone-calls where friends, so-called, had been ranting to her about her husband's 'pretentious' ways. Maryam hadn't known and still didn't know that Yusuf had overheard, and it was true that this wasn't an unusual occurrence in Yusuf's life; people often dubbed him a pretentious man behind his back or over his shoulder. No one had ever said it to his face though, which is what, and quite nicely, again, made the accusations inversions or negative projections of themselves. If it might be true, as Yusuf now supposed the case, a now-convoluted case, that they were being pretentious in their use of that same term, well, then it made sense that none, to date, would (or could) have dared to confront him with the slanderous tag in a way that might allow him to answer the charge, or wipe away, wipe off, the tar of the same. Mar was a nice word, he now thought; whether it did or it didn't, sounding antique, he thought it possessed a King James Bible feel to it, perhaps even Psalm-like. The word smear, too, he thought might be a relative in the eons or ear-like eras of wordy times. But he was no philologist; no; he just had a natural preternatural sense when it came to English words. He'd already read his first words, after all, well before the age of three. It had all started with Joy, his nanny. It was she who'd sat, snug, next to the toddler, Yusuf, as he'd grappled then won with the word 'cow', say, or 'cat', or 'fox', or some version of pastoral that suited a toddler's reading habits. Before 'cow' though, no doubt there had been 'moo'; before 'cat', 'meow'. And so on. It would be slyly pretentious, he now thought, to pretend otherwise.

Joy was a Welsh blond woman. She had brown eyes, a brown though that was right in the starkest middle of brown spectra; which made them indelibly brown against the whites of her big and quite round eyes. And the combination of colours, wheat against chocolate, would continue to sound with fantastic pull throughout Yusuf's later life. But that is neither here nor there; we are concerned here, I believe, with our hero's first efforts, successful by all accounts, at reading English words.

Sat there, on the grainy salmon-pink sofa, they'd been snuggled up in a warming way in Joy's smallish room, whose walls were papered over in sky or baby blue. There was, he remembered, a television in the corner, smallish too, black and square, but still oddly gawky as befitted the mores and fashions of the early eighties of the previous century. It stood about a meter from the inlaid pale blue carpet of the ground, propped by a wooden white structure whose chipped white paint Yusuf could still see in his now adult's mind's eye. And the chipped paint still irritated him, even now. He'd read there as I say of some versions of pastoral; though it was only later, but still not too distant from this toddling time, that he would get to grapple with a certain (or rather, uncertain: and the (eponymous) irony amused him, then as now) number of ambiguities in the modern English canon, or a certain, uncertain, construal of such; the structure of complex words; and perhaps, some quite difficult or at the least determinedly oblique prose on the subject of Milton's God. And Joy was always there to applaud his efforts, then watch the glee multiply on Yusuf's infant face, a vertiginous wizard dancing upon his visage. Which brings us back to that harrying, harrowing, hankering with which we began. Yusuf had always wished for recognition. And perhaps it might be right to say that the womb was never, or would never be, enough.

Prologue

Writing On The Wall

For Faten
Dubai

We have paintings of course, and scented photographs
That smell of the different colours that have coloured
Our pasts. And I have drummed against the walls
As well the biggish bookshelves. The creamy light
From the windows' skies boasts itself, brags itself
As of a better timber than the yellower, less-woodier
Kind the lamps provide. What more, what else? Well…

There are these lines, ascending from the smudgy white
Of my new and old machine – and there is my wife.
And therein lies the lie-less find of my life – there, in
The russet-brown redress, there, the aching redemption.
It's hard to fathom a future farther than this woman;
The bachelor was a mask, always, for the married man –
And I, who have asked all the questions, ask none more.

Disenchantments And Valedictions

A Theory Of Guilt

Dubai

There is a grief I cannot follow.
A reckoning. The walls of my heart are canary-yellow.

This tryst (a fatal dose, my poisoned fellow
Of cowardice) follows me though,

Coupling me without the fruit of that sorrow
Which might have been a comfort.

There are no autumn leaves here, no hurt
Season in this place. Only

The lessening of an unforgiving heat…
And so I cannot leave this place,

Cannot save myself—I'll never grace
My sweaty brow with a tardy stroll, a breeze

Upon my English face. God, I miss
The English weather; its temper, and its pace.

Toyless

Dubai

To haggle and to hedge, and to barter for a life
Can be sad, toyless. The sadness is a sea-long buoy.
It holds burdens, bobbing, weighed like burly gold
In the balancing hand, blinded by passing shoals,
Hurrying past, fluorescent, slim, and screaming
Of their boldness, but viscid as age itself, age
Pricked by slow, falling terror, feeding, fed with rage.

And if I spoke of water, of water in the furlong
Of a different life, pitted now by sores that crow,
Unstitch the long dream-long finger of time
And the mapping drafts that limn and rhyme
In some quick and sullen way, big with wax,
The unearned wages of some slow, daft cliché—
Perhaps I wrote too soon? Perhaps I outbid the moon

In the haggling at this bazaar, its low, strange
Logos of profit and leering? Perhaps it was I
Who failed the gauntlet, the glove, the deftest gear?
There are no twiggy birds in this shadowed place.
There are no naked trees. There is no more, no more
Green, no more green-leafed face. There is only this
Aimless terror, soliciting the weeds of slow and wan disgrace.

The Dark Blue House Of The World

Dubai

I can hear them now, nearing, roomy in their house
Made of a world. They gel, set, emptied noises
Writ to rouse an anger; that of a simpler, clearer creature,
An animal, say, but not a beast, man-like in a snare,
Trapped—the triggered metal, the djinn-spurred errors,
Wrecks to a dream-long gambit that pleaded peace—
Shy now of what might have been, what might have been
Achieved...
                I can hear them in their mansion
Whose bricks are hard, jealous blue—the colour
The night brings like panthers in slipping armies,
A wilderness for a world. And it's a strange grammar
In which to live, breathe, or just for lips to quiver with...

But perhaps it has always been like this: trumpets
Of hate sending hollowed noise, upwards from a cage?

King

Dubai

In what sweetly sovereign land might I rule,
Tossed and yanked, and wrought in a way to be
A sturdy fool, a man of sottish steel?

Year on year, year on year, my kingdom grows
Its scope, fattened to a more swan-like reign,
And the lake does in fact get more placid—

Maddened to a living solid now, mealy-dark, gravid
And sure, bold, still, manned in all but name…

Dominion has its perks, you know,
Mastery, its making. The undulant dead
Upon whom this golden city's built and seen
Are ghosts placed and docked and berthed in me

Like linen; wraiths of passed and livid grey, they air and billow,
Kissing the limbs of this sporting king. It's all so bitterly cruel.

Her Expertise

Of course, it didn't take long in time or long
To expedite the ghost. She shuttled his wise and brawny song
As though it weren't a type of kindness, his brag, his
Boast—in an arc and eon of mostly deftly less.

In short, she slayed, crucified by how she was—
Laying fibs in a square room where no one was
Or dared to be. And the ghost cried wide and long,
Beggaring volume; making poverties, rancid and just,

Of all the long-borne lies. The stink of a well-worn shoe
Echoed and stank, savaged the chrome-white air
To the rank and blue of his lungs and what he knew.
It didn't matter an atom what was true or fair—her

Mockery of the mind was ghost to a ghost; it was everywhere…
And we are razed now, you and I, to a blank tablet; as before.

Questioning Luck,
Or,
Retrodiction

For BK

Recall what the good man said, siphoning
Sweet moneyed laughter on the other end
Of the phone. True, he was a friend,
A good one, too; and true, true, the things
He said were mostly true, reading utmost Zed
From Alpha, and pink from blue. But red
Throats roared that afternoon. He'd said:
You're bound to win the lottery, you're bound to…

And this brings me to the question of luck,
The two angles of vision. *Yes*, giving room
In the past's male house to the given, *yes*,
You might just say things panned-out, kissed.
But what about the given of that devil's muck?
And how about the sterling birth that started
The eventual chains, traitored by the eye? And
The bandwagon of all those years, agonies, blind?

The Mansion Of My Youth

I've never owned a house, of course; the house
That harboured me and where longing dwelled
Was much like a touch of German philosophy—
Not in the musty, fusty sense, but in the grand…

Though it was the home of joy, my joyous sanity,
(Before I'd gallop, whizzing-at the established ease
Of university, where madness waited, an uncoiled
Spring, a faint whiff of tragedy, acids, omens) and though

Lucky to be a girded spirit (given the doe-dear home
Talents)—the only owner's clout I know (arrows, gnomes
And dragons, the sleeker lakes too) is this medalled mind

I love to own. And no market can therein bust, confine
The bursting radiance of a coddled child; a buried child
Whose most inward dwelling grew to weeds and wilds.

His Solitude

Geoffrey Hill, RIP

There's a tall, burly wall between
Loneliness and solitude.

                He spoke

Peerlessly through his palace,
A man bold enough to be
Lean and tortured,
Echoing

In a gilded hall of echoes
A speech that verged and cusped for
The parley of a host
Of very different mirrors—

More grand than grandiose.

He was canny as the snake, footless
With his bone-sunken feet—
His marrow to his bone now's
Seamless, sewn, narrow and neat.

So let the animals now roar: their
Mulching school begins no more—

As one sage goes sagely through the door
To a different place,
A better,

Reflector now of reflector.

The Chants Within Him

Derek Walcott, RIP

He said: 'I know how to sing;
It was I who taught the angels
Bedecking
In happy chains the well-ordered sky.'

And I remember a book of his
In chocolate-brown;
And I recall the flow of oaken sound,
A serried, chanting voice—

For I too was (have been) prodigal…
And now he's gone, passed and dyed
By a chance within him. No gall
Follows him to the grave, no lie.

Valedictions

'… the more perfect the artist the more separate in him
will be the man who suffers and the mind which creates…'
                    T.S. Eliot, 'Tradition and the Individual Talent'

Goodbye to All That

After Robert Graves

Was it war that made you mad, so sadly pickled
With histories? The classics were, had always been
Your deepest keep, car; you kept your secrets there,
Readied to spring from the coil of your mind…

And if to uncoil the What of all of that were
Your girded lesson, for the future to seek and find;
And if to guide us past the hopes of the most salient
Question we try to *Why* the world with, its fickle,
Flippant way—a newer bowel now of unknown pains—

Perhaps the first mythos in your bones was there to say
Goodbye to all of that, and to the marrow, goodbye…

                    *

So. Was it war, at the last, that served to clinch your eyes
To a life of fuller, later pasts, the future mainly, almost blind—

Saying goodbye to all of that, so bitter, brittle, and unkind?

Parade's End

After Ford Madox Ford

It took you, friend, a clutch of years to find the way
To wall, confine the pain of those bitter, brittle days,

Those bright claps of pounding noise, the infernal play
Whose drama had no woe-sweet, rue-sweet recognitions…

And later: your high and haughty hero, a chap deftly-flawed by
The ball-and-chain by which you had his mind downed, weighted;

And later: the lithe and limpid run of that clean-run girl, woman,
With whom he fell, and loved, began a little whimper, touched

Enough to cry… *Yes, it took a while*: to deaden the dead who'd
Peopled your fractioned, fractured mind; and perhaps the ditch

Of that muddy time was a gap aptly-needed—to be burrowed by
The later writer, the later scribe, the later, and fuller mind?

Perhaps the term it took to find your end, the pen's parade,
Was a licit time; later lit-up by later; and the god of all you made?

Pangloss

Dubai

Sometimes, in the work of an early morning minute,
I will think-through the unoiled cogs of the disaster
By which manacles hinged to the sometime-laughter
Of a loved life less loved—when the ominous spirit

Daggered cleaner waters, softly-fingered childhoods,
Honing to an undulant valley whose darkened goods
Were two hills that touched and kissed at their base—
And think of how sadness might be a permanent place;

But think of how the weeping-joy in my new-born's face
May remedy all, turning youths into arcs of adulthood;
And how the swell of that ruddy text for the reading eye
May line their lines with a kind and glazy softness. And I

Winter my wits, once burdened with that bony sadness—
Choosing to un-remember the Life in a life's dun remit.

Greybeard

Smoking-Area B at AUD

The bare boughs are nimble, slim, and dressed in
Scarecrow-grey, as though aching beards inhered within.
Knots in the barks' middles are knotty-grey
Conflations, the trapped energies of the trees
Find their sunny docks there, inwards, where
The grey torture goes mentored, and begins…

Youths flame their pipes, sat on the roseate bench,
And gabble and gabble: pig-Latin, Emirati-Mensch…
I was young once; and once, my own dapper absence;
And I too, I too fired the Self that I
Found in me, berthed like them: mellow, tense,
And full of the cryptic question. Why,

Past now the dead leaves, the grey dilapidation,
Do I turn again to stone—my own mote, my own nation?

Dawn Music, Dubai

Sky-black: a bird, a carrion-bird has died.
She was picking her way through the utter field
Of the dead, a darned precious vulture in her head,
When she was asked by the living God to kneel

To the same old dying carousel of us all…
And the wide gamut of the sinning dead stirred
Their limbs to the feel of that happy loss…

Just so, the cursed equations I must cross
To matter from a rabid, avid rubbish this
Dawning dare (a piece of downy music) are absurd.

For it's too early to be waking / to be heard —
Busy with my lyre, and laying out the cost
Of this sky-black and darkened funeral
Of what seems like the cloth of a death-dyed world.

Cowardice At The Confessional

Dubai

One day you will be gone, coloured into nothing,
And the service of all my questions—that beckoning
Like a blanket that slides over my knees and chest
Back and forth, back and forth—will be a prayer

To one at rest. And to live with that beleaguered
Thought, battling the mind like a spur to confess
To what I can't confess, never doing what was done
In the judgments of the arrows of a world at one,

To live like that, thinking of naught when I have
Everything a man could want, life, health, love,
And a mind so quick it bickers with quickness

And whatever else a man might mean to possess
In the way of true deep grip—to live like that,
Knowing the end, might be to fear the sea for its wet.

The Desert

Dubai

Perhaps the sand was an afterthought?
The odd palm tree, I know, sprinkling a spare
Parcel of ground with shade,
Was not made in quietness for one such as me.

And you can ask the white-hot sky about it—
Sweltering, as it will, with the image of its own
Talent for baking illusions
In the sweat-lit realm of our minds.

For the sky's a narcissist like no gloating other.
He will batter you with the idea
That you are something you are not, deep down
Knowing the wile and maelstrom, his own

Flagellating desire to be, just that, stet, equally.
Here in the desert there is no spring of feeling,
Only a numbness; laid in the colour of a bruise,
Still it somehow stings. I have no simple news.

The Evil Eye

Dubai

She believes it's there, a pincer movement
Ratcheted and ratcheting a small effort of air.

Battlements are no use, she avers. *The turrets
You speak of,* she says, *they're zeroes within snares
Of more. It picks apart the worst men from
The best men, lugging and luring and lulling the latter
Till they're worsted.* She believes it's there,
*And whether you pluck or plug, the beaten sum
Remains the same: for every green—a sourness
Proffered; for each sap, and the very destinies of clear
Water—the darts and daggers on the tongue of lime.*

My wife is wiser than me in many different ways,
But in the same cave-life we all seem to profess—
Plato's mythos still weighs with a certain age.

Love Songs And White Goddesses

The Nile Farewell

'And neither can be certain who
Was that I whose mine was you.'
				Robert Graves, 'The Thieves'

She leaves me love as I leave her,
Two inklings in a mind that's shared—
Skin to fur and fur to bear... There's

A wise skin-brown inside the gambit
Of these readied lives—it splays as it sits
Here in a tan café by the Nile... Meanwhile,

The ochre bulge of buildings, shoulders
Tumbling to the precipice of an antique Egypt,
Are brownish boulders: squat, square, fat

And burly shoulders bent upon this curve
Of the big river... The breeze here shines
As though it were a piece of the afternoon

Sun, the lazy gusts of the sweet Nile air
Are like our love—a heat that rounds to care
To cool... So, we bid farewell—the Nile, her

Lean, suave motion, ripples: silvery, grey and green—
A waxwork to forge her native, motive sheen;
Platinum a plant on gunmetal.

The Pledge

For Faten

Her words are like towers
To sacrifice their stone;
Her words are like oaths

Pledged in some brittle nation
Where true and false are both
Petals on the same damned flower…

Rocks weep from my eyes.
Metal blisters
From the shield

I wield—
A round of clay
To defend and dye

The clay-red earth
I walk upon. And I feel the gel
And molding; and I feel

The poet at the potter's wheel—
While he shapes his real, his
Own special pattern of bliss…

And there is so much tooth
In that ceramic; and there is
So much of deadened use…

At the last, she remains
A fountain whose water
Counters the ghosts

Big with bulky slaughter
In a hermetic mind. And
The fruit of him has rind.

Loving Vincent

For Faten

The licks and daubs may flicker, savagely true,
And she has loved the show.

Scores of artists lend their ears, ears like canny doors,
And the whore at the source of the question

Finds a heap to listen to—bleeding there, red, and listening.
And if I were to cut my own, like some cheap, solicitous drone

Faced by an artist, sweatier, whose right was rightly wrong—
I'd see my song less deftly dreamy; for I love his knightly hue,
                                        pricked by drunken stars.

In the cinema of our lives, in the desert of the same,
My love has more panache

In the name of her better name. I cannot slash
Across a canvas with such visceral, filmic truth—

My licks, my daubs are meager; they serve to serve the reign
Of the radical wand-strokes of a madly better man.

The Woman Hungers For Drama,
The Man Hunts For Peace

The air was doing cartwheels the while,
The gulls caterwauled in white carousels
And a fisherman in a Bedouin robe
Proffered his hand of help. Our road
Through the antique city of camel-
Colored stones, past the hive that glowed
Amber, the rock-innards of a mosque,
Was far from rocky; it was more like silk...

The aged gambits there—the sky-wide gamut
Of guests, who strove to canter and to care
For the tauter wits of an older, haler center;
Such marvels, and better conduits towards
The core, the keystone, the loadstone of what
To be there, or here, might come to mean,
Much as it once did—the air being ridden by mint
Striations... And it was Bedouin fare, as though color

Came served to the journeyed eye: warm as lard,
A hospitable mess... The drama, the adventure
Thrilled her—you know: the widening of the scope...
The while, the man stayed in the jungle of his
Conceit, hunting like a mane for his lioness
After the bitter gold for a smidgeon of peace...
The woman there hungered to dye all with risk;
The man was happy, mote-happy, with a simpler silk.

Three Sonnets For Faten

1. The Positive Sum

Seated for dinner in Rome, oh, two years back,
The evening smelt in puma, food on the way while
I dressed you with a streak of felt, a deep-borne
Silk—my words climbed then soared about the sky
Of what was now well-meant between us, by
And bye. The sentence or two or three I used
Showed a positive sum had now become my muse.
I said something like this, bloody but tender, real:

Tomorrow, if I die, return to He Who recollects—
At the least I'll have lived, for a short while, anyway,
With love in my life. Dying tomorrow, shall we say, may
Cap or boss this quiet, rest, the arc and boon, now as then,
Of a good life, better, best—we cohere to the call: Pleromatic…

And you smiled in velvet, finished, sutured, sealed.

2. Her Reading Glasses

A knowing look like a noun on her face,
She dons her reading glasses;
Only to unveil this elfish grace—

A deuce of dimples, ratcheted by a smile,
A grin at work that limns a style
Of being placid, well…

What she sees perhaps I have, too.
She reads from a smallish oblong screen,
Snug, pillowed, abed—the two of us like two

Lives as much to be and be as been…

Desire here speaks, but as a clot and map of needs—

And I am braille to her while she is blind
And she's a thoughtful dwelling I read
In some arcane philosophical mind.

3. Loving Puritans

In the gradual working of a love there are many fountains:
The first plunges, gallops down, like a water of women;
The second may be a spray, a little spittle, frittering the mien
To a space where wet, whether whiter or grey, meets ocean-
Deeps; the third, let's say, is the love between puritans…

We do not ask the weather of the minds of our loved ones
Without a little madness, touched; such dark trepidation
Teeters on the balls of heartfelt feet when souls are sane.
Tonight, it was like, for the first time, I asked her name,

And she replied that it was different. The same lending
You give to an errant beggar, the same good and selfless song
By which you part with a small, brash token of your wrongs—

Such was I tonight… And though she is my deftest rhyme,
We spoke in tongues tonight, differently slipping as the same.

Adeodatus

For Maha Faris Sabbagh

I see her again, the girl with the cream-white skin
And the Oryx-eyes; the girl whose emerald gaze
Led her up a winding mountain village road
To a place of worship that was foreign to her

And to the heritage of her kin. She wishes there, in
Her most vital self, to obey—perchance to please
The god who was a very foreign-looking god,
Pinioned there, as though hacked by vultures.

What was the girl doing there? Many asked.
What steep beveling in the spirit had led her
There? What great, wide pinion of pitting Grace?
But her eyes washed themselves, and basked

In the sense of glory buried deep and within
The suffering of him—the son of a god / of a man
And woman; the son she felt stir within, a rumbling
In the tummy, boding ill for good. Boding utter song.

The Silent Oryx

For Maha Faris Sabbagh, on her birthday

In a small, warm corner of this place
A bunch of mint ascends, wafts like wraiths and glowing embers

Neither green nor white; they're like a baffled, unknown race
Of lovers in graceful carousels who serenade the mute and naked air;

And in the small, warm silence it makes amends
For all that made much and so little sense. That said, though,

Your mothering was a flame of a stamp that was always so
Mysterious, smoke in the bones of your emerald gaze…

It is autumn now. And now in the autumn of your days
May the coming of winter be and be and be, happy, capricious—

Some girlish, twirling summer dress
Beneath the beelines and the golden emanations;

Some girlish warmth, let's say; and (salmon-thick) a smile that may
Confess the Care was worth it, building children, burning nations.

Heartbeat

Clutch and release, grasp, clinch and let-go
In a small part of this curving parcel of life,
Black and thorough in the frame of the machine

Needling an eye through the seamless pouring
Of love twined by two—I sing my first and my
Final song, a lyric I hear on a harp without strings.

All my nightmares have led to the dream of you;
All the lived, the viscid horrors, turn at the beauty
Of one who cannot be anything as yet, but true

As nightfall and sunrise, the light at its seam,
The bright corner where all things are enough, this choir
Of one violin, and a drum and a pea-small sound

Like the gabbling of gold from a golden halo. Half-
Moon, beloved nut—never was anything so round
As you, who walk down the leaf-strewn avenue of

The daft and singular cleverness of your mother
And I; the womb of your sturdiest ground, the bard
Quick to lose his tune, poor before the price of words.

A Daughter

For Faten

The wild cry of this undulant night
Whose blue's more silver than purple
Slides like a voice in search of signs
Like words, foils of the brave sublime—
The flesh of many minds like symbols.

I can't find a straight, untethered line
Except in her, and the unchained sounds
Of my future—the night is white with a girl…

And then I look to my left, to my right,
Seeing things like glossy marbles
Strung to build my rope of time; to lull
The knot that signs at the knotty middle—

Unravelled now by a carrying wife
Whose care holds more than unskinned love.

The Ballerina

For my daughter, womb-dwelling
Dubai

It's a bit like a book, this passage of sleep.
Between two covers you find you reach
Into bigger or more and different worlds,
Such as this one, these, where my daughter is.

*

As spring steps up her springy force, a girl
Wonders into life, kicking and dancing,
Her mind, already touched:
                        the ballerina.
The sounding force of her operatic heart,
Rhapsode She…
                And to speak again
Of that paper dream, to let words exist there,
Might be to find that slipping, unstuck moment
When a page turns, doing its fluttery business
Of Page…

And I won't be told a bedtime story
Because of her. And I won't be gifted that
Ancient arc of light one speaks of, looking backwards,
Remorse a kind of gluttony, inching into eras.
And I won't awake to the bitter night at night
Because of what a father possesses.

I will be there.

And I will be there,
Aching like this happy ghost
Who sees his child timed by the eyes of angels.

*

So, sleep on. Kick on. Be avid in the womb
Of your watery stillness. Be true
In that way of yours I seem to know,
Awake to all that's soft, aglow, and tender.

Reflections

White Noise

Dubai

Strange to say it, but I've a nose for such things,
Smelling the whiteness, greenness, and so on…

I teach Plato, for instance, and the platonic folly
Of seeing that you see, the light, the lightest worry,

And I dance across the stage of the dapper class
Raging wrongs, kinds of error, lessening in kindness,

And I dance like the eye does / like the other one,
Too, where two eyes make one, make two, make

That seam that seams like with like, with unlike.
And with unlike, I teach my pupils to grow, blacker

And blacker, till they return to their origin of white.
I've a nose for such things, though it's strange to say it.

And the white noise, and the white noise muddles along
To the middle of the flesh that meets the dark laughter.

Beirut Rain

A frond beneath my window tussles with the wind.
The wind by turns tussles with the burden of its own daft sins.
And such duplicity serves.
The rain in a Beirut winter is like the glamour of the people

Of Beirut in a Beirut winter:
Samurais and yogi, kamikazes in the blend
Of the acts of loud or quiet immolations…
What's infolded here unfolds, here as much as elsewhere—

Coils finding hapless births inside their springs,
Portents finding omens inside themselves…
I wish I could return a sewn-sad bunch
Of pasts to some high shelf

In the bookshop of my body's learning.
But I cannot. All that's swappable, possible,
Is short shrift, touched song. A way of thinking, a way of going
On, gifting the madness of a history flesh it never had.

General Knowledge: An Elegy

Dubai

When you died, daggered by the rounder compass of
A world of queer and slier norths— seeing things beneath
A commanding order now,
                              forging a fist of worth
From the shame of severed fingers, out of viscid mess
Finding the hand that guides, finding a hand's caress—

When you died, and I saw the white starkly in the black
Of the pupils of your eyes (closed, sewn students now)

And saw the bitterness woven like a hymn, a choric
Stage, to be acted, sung, proudly from your quiet brow;
When you died, the sum of all my knowledge proved

As nothing, and the gears, and the knives of all my gifts
Meant nothing now, a few pennies in a currency, leaking, loud
But obsolete— dead the tree of any burst, any better song…

And much of me died with you, you who were never wrong.

On Digging

For my father, Mohamad Sabbagh
Dubai

He passed many years ago, now, parked and glossed.
I teach his poems nearly every day. I trust the sparks
Of all his embers still glow, glimmer; I have to.

And through the eddies, the heartening ebb and flow
Of the rug and weave of all this time, textures passed
In the company of the angles of the angel-dark,

I have realised a truth filled with the violin's mark—
You know, the unlucky one, sublime, perhaps, a thorough
One that lasts. The years since have lifted the curse

And I feel better speaking to you now. The rasp
Of all the digging done, now as then, then as now,
Comes up twenty years away— and the effect, filmic

As it ever was. In this sunk, son-bit movie, though,
The emanations revolve; beams turned upwards, they ask.

Father To Father

Dubai

Because of the way, the rampant, tortured way
The skeins of our pasts turned into hurricanes;

Because, that is to say, of the syllabic way
The planets happened into orbit, forming a crucial stain

From darkly stellar distances
Upon the wage we used to keep about our name—

Spending it, but thriftily, shall we say,
Scrimping the coin of a taut, tutored, handsome bliss—

Because of all of this; because of all that was precious
To us, grooming and slaking and feeding us

From the udder of a loved necessity;
Due to many things, things that were messy and things that were gritty

Coming to replace the choice exempla we were wrought to see
As parts of grace— because of this, and these, perhaps…
                              perhaps we are the same.

Two Edifices

1 A Building's Weave

After a Thomas Heatherwick building, South Africa

Picture her past, this hive of light and glass;
the way it spurred helpmeets to the people, maize
and flour— and needs before
                              slingshots of desire…

There were no split tongues, and no
echolalia there

and all it took, with a steady gaze and with
steady flair—
                    building inside from out gifts
of love-work, bulwarks and birds
filled with futures and objects for words—

and all it took
was a give to her bellied guts her
honour's due…

*

                    Here, in a library of stone
and glass,
                    the mind
                    of the architect's
a mind at work / at play in a text of bones—

and here
                    the art's

glamour's flex and thought
are pasts
in a space of futures wrought,
forged—

                    hollowing to a prayer
far stronger
                    because it asks

of solid things that are solid.

2 EMBA

*After the new Executive MBA building at AUD
Dubai*

It starts with light, the cool flame of an idea…
Late winter, and the sun's coil starts its glances,
Slow to unspring in mellow tones her white on glass…

The sheer inkling of flow, flow without fat here—
It springs from a sum of squarish dwelling, an edifice
Where markets of the mind will clutch, will grasp at

A thing which goes, goes, an economy of scale,
Shall we say, and the unflinching gloss that sees
Finites merge through moves that are— as infinite

As the world presently is… This block of white
Future; this limpid run, running-through; this fight for
Winnings, touched to be's, rare ambitions—and being: filled

By desire's good, desire's bad; these ranks of flair
To be crunched in a building's flourishing business
With the gathering of knowledge in the solitary air.

Delusions

After Nadine Labaki's Capharnaum

If you stroll, amble, as we did, into the theatre—

A different mode of walking will grip your legs
When you depart, hams like big, round tears
Working the tissue. Leaving, your eyes ended, you'll renege
All the films you may have watched, gladly-eliding

By the same grand, world-tutored sleep
That goes to make our daily, blinded, common song…

And the closing curtain may be fine: but it's you, ripped
By welling thanks that are far from the unformed sounds
Of your neighbour's weeping, caught brittle, found
Out, a good woman, made much worse of a sudden…

And as we wake here from the warmed and lifelong sun
Of our dreams, let us recollect our beginnings—
Naked once, bawling, purple, wet; and the fear

We might've felt back then, and the wordless rear
Of our starting lives—even that was near to bliss
When compared to just a small smattering of this.

Guessing At A World

For Said Durra
Dubai

In Lebanon, years ago,
I turned a chalk-white face to a friend.
I was guessing, and so I said—

Speaking from wheels or tamer cogs
But still unfree—

That it, the world, I meant, just couldn't be.

His smile was a brimming jug.

And so, as though

The native mint, thyme, of that un-green city
Turned, and suddenly,
Into trust
Like wafts of simple truth—

You know, the plinth, the pyre,
The neater periods
Of breathing
The breath of a classical ideal—

As though the daftness of so many centuries
Coped with, written in the stars
Of some deceit

Turned its face—clever now
And big enough to wane
To clarity and its smaller fame

Of a minute.
His name was Said, like my brother's.

And if I were to guess again,
Trying to pin more than
To pinion,

I would say it one more time:

We live worlds in our lives,
And the world itself could never be
What we feel it
To be.

Growing Up

Dubai

Seated at brunch, the food, an agony of plenty,
It becomes clearer and clearer which way
The years went. Tabled there, the close-call
Of a few, the djinn can till what the djinn can tell—

And a rhapsode rates the tale, a summed dark smudge
Of dun and blue. So much for Saturn, or *way back when!*
So much for the exigent self—his flagellating rues
Are small round cakes gone nibbled by a child in this

Same pattern of paths, simple, quick, just a little bit lost…
Or perhaps not? Perhaps the easier answer is, and is
The better one? Perhaps that small and glossy pin one
Pins to one's chest, feeling safer with the effortless

Banal, touchstones, the dreary axioms, pat, automatic—
Perhaps to sing like that's not the mean, dumb project
I take it for? Perhaps they've a different name for day?
Or perhaps they sleep at night like judges judged

Too? Filled with acres and angles, the infinite crew?
I'd like to grow up; but there are no more years to add
In the canon of number. He plays a smooth mathematics
Without a bluff through all His sadness, does God.

Epilogue

The Clown And The Philosopher

Beirut, Lebanon
For TA

I must not walk today, because walking is a must;
To move at all in a naked world like this must mean to trust.

There is a small, tin voice in me, the shard of a philosopher;
He speaks a clutch of things to a private world, but doesn't care,

At the last, for me… Streets below the window of my mind
Shriek and shout; the quest-shaped sage opines slow motes: *they're being kind*,

He says. Then a man walks past the window, toking upon his phone,
And the clown inside avers a jest, the rapid joke of his opinion,

While doing cartwheels from a thick, rouged mouth
Uttering words that spoil and hold no farther south

Than this: *my friend and I, a friend whom you call the philosopher,*
Well, we do this twinning thing, this pas a deux, this dancing square,

A minuet, if you like—but only because the two of us, halves of you,
Wish to make the trip unpassable: for none to believe the truth. And you,

I know, will now descend to the maelstrom of some cheapish poem:
But that means little to us; we only speak with dying Romans

And you are not one such—a lazy kind of lout, a smaller kind of coward.
And you may reply in many English tongues, your burly words

Like cellos, perhaps, but still, none will buy the creed of you:
You've worked and slacked, grinding, lax—so long, making blue into better blue—

And now it's time; time's great fetter lands, like a rodent-bird, on the sill of your life;
Lands, perched like a nervy squirrel, shivering for a nut, a long slim knife

Seeming to slice the young chap in two.
And all the world will say, again and again: and who, and who are you?

Afterword

My Practice of Poetry, Or, Not Bad

Nearly all of the poetry that comprises this collection was written within the space of half an hour, if not less—and very rarely ever revisited. It's not so much that I don't believe that care should be taken when trying at least to write good verse, as that by temperament I am impulsive, impatient and lucky enough to have a facility with language and the configuration of senses that allows me to write, on occasion, good verse quickly and easily. Put another way (and as will be clear to any canny reader of this collection), it's not really the stories I have to tell that count in my poetry; firstly, because being lyrical and confessional most of the time, those stories tend to be just about me—and for all my insightfulness (ponce that I am), there's nothing particularly special about me; but secondly, because when I write the urgency is sourced, as far as I can tell, in the need to effect an artefact that evinces control, which is to say, some type of formal discipline—and not in the urgency of a tale that really needs telling. Putting borders round a sentiment or a unified block of them gives me pleasure, and my hope is that there's a chance that that practice may give an equal pleasure to the right kind of reader. It's not so much about the garden, then, as much as it's about the rigor and flow in the happiness of gardening. I, I, I, yes; but also: it remains the case that at my best, as I hope anyway, that that egotism is married to a kind of embodiment that is probably more (or perhaps, just as much) instinctual and sourced in pre-verbal experience. These pieces, beyond all the detritus in the middle which has been excised, hopefully, from the book's collating, arrived like they were meant to be—bodies of God, so to speak, rather than dogs-bodies. And if I tend to be highly responsive to the paraphernalia and the rigmarole of relationships, that's because my efforts at empathy are probably reaction formations to the aforementioned ego-centrism. And yes, I, I, I (again); indeed, such late (late, late) romanticism is probably out of fashion, and (maybe rightly) deemed in bad taste. Freud, too, I gather is outdated. But then, the bubble in which the gestalt of my-self was formed—upper-middle-class, privileged in so many ways, effortlessly literate, articulate—was always going to be the equivalent (or simulacrum) of 1895 bourgeois Vienna. I leave it, then, to some souped-up social theorist in the far future, digging up slim and disregarded tomes in some fusty library, to formulate how my apolitical (ahistorical) verse is actually doing politics—but by means of some arcane mediation or some Byzantine chiasmus. The older I get, and quite like a good romantic, the more reflectively conservative I become. If I have suffered, it was and is probably for good reason; if I have written any decent verse, that, too, probably has some brilliant logic to it. Not everyone can be a hero, though heroes are no doubt good; but still: that doesn't mean that not being a hero, one is bad. The superordinate comes to the (now-mediated) rescue, as always, for the slowly-morphing conservative (or what one might classify, alternately: a principled laziness). Words like yellow, say, only have what I believe is called by logicians an 'external negation', namely: 'not yellow.' (That said, a student informs me that the opposite of yellow is indeed: 'purple.' Though that no doubt only pushes the logical problem one stage further back, as the whole color-scale itself needs must be as much a construction as any haler concept.) But I'm waffling again. To be short and just—put it this way: if my verse is not quite good enough to be ranked in the top-tier of contemporary practice, it is perhaps because, after living through personal, infernal harrows, I have chosen to ratify what came naturally anyway, namely, to cultivate my private garden.